First Published in 2020 by R

Cover photo and design Debbie Ross

The right of Debbie Ross to be identified as the author of this work has been asserted in accordance with the Copyright, Designs and Patents Act 1988.

Debbie was given her first typewriter at the age of 11 and has been writing poetry, short stories and articles ever since - publishing her first article in 1979.

Born in London, but now living on a hill overlooking the Cromarty Firth, near Inverness in the Highlands, Debbie spent 15 years working in the third sector. She now works for herself, baking bread for local community markets. An enthusiastic blogger, along with writing, Debbie enjoys photography, gardening, arts & crafts and open water swimming. She is a keen proponent of all things 'green'.

Debbie's poetry has appeared in magazines and anthologies and been placed in competitions. This is her first published collection.

Immersion

The action of immersing someone or something in a liquid.

Deep mental involvement.

Immersion

Debbie Ross

Ross Cottage Publishing

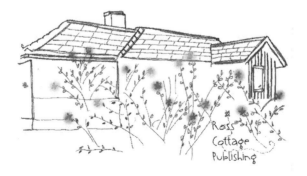

For Tony

Acknowledgements

My thanks to Cynthia Jones Rogerson, who ran the creative writing group at Eden Court, for encouraging me to keep writing at a time when I had almost given up. To our splinter group, 'The Small Group of Love', who were always supportive and happy to share feedback; to my good friend 'Peu' (Paula Harmon) whose positivity and determination has convinced me to be braver and to my husband Tony, who is always supportive and practical, and without whom this volume would be a poorer offering.

Contents

Water Baby

I was born to water
like some people
are born to fame.

Dragged screaming
from amniotic fluid,
I knew the solidity of land
was not for me.

My parents sensed it -
launched me in water
at an early age -
feeling perhaps,
my callipered legs
would quickly turn
to mermaid's tail.

I swam,
to save myself
from drowning.

And still
the living water calls me;
keeping me
coast-bound -
the necessity of sea.

Farewell To Skye

Purple-hazed mountains,
a water-colourists smudge
on the skyline.

Your crags and cliffs
engirdling,
tempting the risk-takers
and unwary.

Centuries of defences
breeched
in a single charge
of iron and steel -
buckled to the mainland;
island now
in none but name.

Beach Dancers

Moving silently to a symphony
of wind and waves,
you mark your steps in the sand.
Oblivious to dog walkers and curious children,
amused onlookers to your seashore salsa.

A British Climate

(for Pat Patel)

It was too much -
the responsibility for new life;
with no support
and the weather:
the rain incessant,
June unseasonably cold.

It was too easy
to throw away her life;
with no support
and the weather:
constant downpours,
the forecast worse to come.

It's all too much -
caring for this new life;
with no support, no wife,
and this tragic weather.

Off to bluer skies,
the weather more like home;
sunshine a better omen
for new beginnings.

Environmentally Friendly

The writer
is an environmentalist by nature,
storing each experience for future plot;

keenly preserving
the landscape
in detailed observation;

never wasting
a single impression,
recording the lot.

You never know
when you'll be able to
recycle it -
especially in a poem!

Battle Ground

He whipped her
with wild words,
tongue thrusting arrows at her heart;
delivering his attack
in measured mouth-sized missiles;
battering her with sound.

She sat quietly,
clutching at his heart;
stoning him with silence
and battlements of no response;
building an armoury of passive resistance,
silence crushing back.

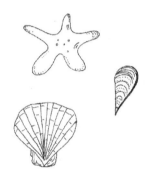

Magpie

She gathers shells from the seashore,
glass and wood and stones.
She hoards shiny treasures from junk shops,
charity shops and garage sales.
She gathers sparkling things
that mean nothing,
and everything.

She stores up, in her heart,
the little tokens that prove your love;
lays them out forensically -
evidence, not sentiment.

I Used To Wish I Were Bobby Charlton

It's not that you *minded* girls;
boys seemed simpler then
and more robust,
a lot less trouble later on.

It isn't that you *wanted* boys -
a desire for offspring fit and healthy;
good hand-to-eye co-ordination
and a fervent love of football, cricket, bowls;
someone not me -
head in the clouds and a love of poetry.

We loved the tomboy foolery when we were young;
balls thrown high in practice-catch;
homemade rounders, and cricket on the beach,
though we were never destined
to be sporting superstars.

The bits of paper meant nothing to you;
no substitute for shield or silver cup,
local back-page statistics, and Saturdays at the club.

I used to wish I were Bobby Charlton,
or Georgie Best;
any sporting god would do.

These days I don't bother with the tennis tournaments
or swimming galas - always last;
not hiding behind the veneer of competition,
simply needing to be loved
by you.

The writing will never count:
a 'runner-up' or 'commended' will never be enough.
No longer trying to achieve to please
I'm freed to fail - or win.
A sporting super-hero is easy to admire;
I hope it's me you love....

Page left intentionally blank

Immersion

Icy fingers needle,
pricking up goosebumps.
The shock
of cold, stealing breath,
coming in gasps.
And then
you're in,
slicing through cold -
sparkling silver, green, blue.
Limbs heavy, head numb,
caught in the moment;
hearing only water, feeling water,
seeing water,
absorbed in the loch, the moment:
immersed.

Dawn Chorus

Missiles of geese crack
the waking sky with their charge of chatter;
the crows strike up a cacophony
of noisy squabbles for a roost;
an oystercatcher -
at the wrong end of his day -
shrills his 'pic-pic-pic'
above the crowd
and gulls in ones and twos
join the melee with their raucous shouts.
A wary blackbird trills alarm,
and collared doves "ru-hoo ru ru-hoo"
as they take heed and fly.
The garden birds in ensemble, singing,
as the new dawn breaks.

Highland Haiku Quartet

Tearing at fodder
A steaming scrum of highlands
lumbering lazy.

                    Buzzards mewl above
                    high in the summer thermals,
                    coasting to a meal

Winter hay away,
grass still left for sheep to graze -
nature's resilience

                    Weed seeds and insects
                    mingle in the autumn breeze -
                    farewell to summer

Ness

The headlights shine bright on the river
as it heads on its weary journey;
taking away the sadness, turning it to light
in the bright ocean sway of the sea;
rhythmic, not rushing, its slow
constant pace finally shedding the pain.

The toil and the ferment, the pain
is the same, all carried away by the river.
Every battle and famine in slow
churning streams all journey
their way to the sea.
All are turned into sand in the light.

Relentlessly winding its way into light,
peat-burdened with sorrow and pain,
Ness makes its inevitable way to the sea.
Centuries of wearing through rock, the river
is powerful and eager, its journey
can take forever, no one can say it is slow.

Meander or hurry it's constant through time, slow
and evolving its shadow and light;
In moonlight and sunlight the journey
is made, with delight and with sorrow, with joy or
with pain.
Industrious water, calmer of fears; the river
unceasing, its unbroken drive to the sea.

Take me and change me in depths of the sea,
unchanging guardian of the slow
moving story; hail tributary, Ness, the river.
Ripple and bathe me in glorious light,
wash away sadness and pain,
let me joy again in the journey.

I watch from the window, your journey
unending, meandering calmly your path to the sea.
I feel all the black weight of watery pain
and the burden you bear for our slow-witted clan;
Ness full of beauty, Ness full of light;
I watch and marvel, you sparkling river!

The headlights shine bright on the river, its journey
of light to the glittery sea.
So slow we are to realise
the pain and the depths that you carry.

Page left intentionally blank

The Duck

Bill and feathers
in noisy commotion
for manna thrown by a child.

My duck sits out the melee,
paddling casually to retain
his place by the bank;

iridescent jade and blue,
the male mallard glints in sun and water
as he dunks
and bobbles up again;
then, nibbling at the current,
tilts his head to swallow.

He laughs his "mwaq, mwaq, mwaq"
deep and guttural,
stretching out his wings
with a shimmy and shake of water.

The female blinks,
ignores his clamorous display -
water off a duck's back.

Down To The Sea

I thought it would be good
to go down to the sea;
to wreck the torment inside
with the tempest.

Alas, my head was full
of more than cobwebs
and nothing blew away,
save salt tears in sea-spray.

Beachcomber

Detritus spewed up on sand and stone:
the storm trees and driftwood,
the obligatory beer cans;
Nike trainers separated
by time and tide;
a football deflated -
dreams waterlogged or abandoned;
yards of rope made useless
by tangled time
and nets too ragged to mend;
plentiful plunder
for the artist, the poet.

H2O

We think that we control
the flow
by turning the tap.
We're powerless to command
the touch-and-go of energy:
a cloudburst-downpour-wave of life
or death.

Thank you for buying this book. You can connect with Debbie on Twitter @DRnaturegirl, on Instagram drnaturegirl and via her website https://www.debbiemross.co.uk/

If you have enjoyed this collection, please consider leaving a review.

Printed in Great Britain
by Amazon

18822942R00032